CONTENTS

READING, WRITING, OH WHAT FUN!

FROM THE FOUNDER

by: CJ IVES LOPEZ

Issue #9 is about diversity and inclusion. Throughout history, one person, group, or organization has tried to keep someone out of the equation. I want to celebrate how far we've come as a society and how far we must go.

Finding a way to understand each other and work together is at the core of human decency because none of us gets out of here alive.

Throughout time literature has celebrated our differences uniquely and brought these differences into our homes, teaching us how to accept the uniqueness of indivudliasm. This issue is at the heart of that concept.

I found four authors with books celebrating diversity and inclusion to demonstrate how literature can bring forth works of art with profound messages and entertainment to break open conversations that some try to push under a rug.

I hope you enjoy all of these books. Give them a read when you can and open the dialogue within yourself on the biases that you may not realize you have.

Until next time my friends, enjoy the ride.

Meet us at The BookFest

April 1st & 2nd

The BookFest Spring 2023 Adventure features an amazing lineup of authors and literary speakers.

For more information about the speakers and their books, go to The BookFest website. And don't forget to sign up to receive the virtual gift bag filed with special offers and deals from BookFest sponsors.

View the full schedule and plan your BookFest weekend at:
HTTPS://WWW.THEBOOKFEST.COM/KEYNOTE-PANELS-SPRING-2023/

The BookFest is the Webby Award-Nominated platform that brings together readers, authors, agents, celebrities and industry professionals. It is a livestream event that happens in Spring and Fall.

WWW.THEBOOKFEST.COM

JZEPHYR'S CURSE: A GRIMOIRE CHRONICLES NOVELETTE

Zelda Knight is a USA Today bestselling author of steamy romance, a British Fantasy Award-winning, and NAACP Image Award-nominated editor, and a diverse bookseller.

She's also the publisher and editor-in-chief of Aurelia Leo, an independent Nebula Award-nominated press.

Zelda co-edited Dominion: An Anthology of Speculative Fiction from Africa and the African Diaspora (Aurelia Leo, 2020), which has received critical acclaim, and Africa Risen: A New Era of Speculative Fiction (Tordotcom, 2022).

Keep in touch on social media @AuthorZKnight.

Visit her website https://authorzknight.com/

Email z@authorzknight.com

ZEPHRY'S CURSE CONT'D

When did you start writing?
I started writing when I was very young. My first finished story was a self-insert magical girl adventure. Haven't stopped ever since!

What was it like growing up?
Moving around a ton when I was little meant I was generally stuck in my book worlds/fantasy land, as it was hard to make friends in each new town and state. But overall, I had a very happy childhood.

How was your early life?
I would say my early life was very chill, other than my Mom's health. She got diagnosed with autoimmune diseases young, which impacted me for obvious reasons.

What has been the biggest influence in your career?
Discovering the wealth of Black lit out there, full stop. From classics such as Toni Morrison's The Bluest Eyes to the steamiest indie paranormal romance, it opened my eyes to the fact that I could write protagonists that look and talk like me in genres I already adored.

Tell us about your newest release.
My newest release at the time of writing this interview is Pack Queen, a reverse harem omegaverse romance featuring Charity, a rare shifter, who meets three fated mates.

Which book of yours would you call your favorite child?
Probably Percy Jackson & the Olympians though I had a ton of favorites, not even counting comics.

What inspired you to write this book?
Pack Queen is a part of one of three romance universes I'm building: Atherverse (Omegaverse), Astral Mates (Sci-Fi Romance), and Arcane Grimoire (Urban/Paranormal Fantasy). So, Pack Queen came about as an addition to the other omegaverse romances, in which society is divided into three class Alpha/Beta/Omega. I explain more about the concept here on my blog: https://authorzknight.com/what-is-omegaverse/. If you want a free story, check out Zephyr's Curse: https://authorzknight.com/arcane-grimoire-series/, a part of the Arcane Grimoire Universe. What can go wrong when a curious crow shifter finds a rare grimoire? You can find out by signing up for my newsletter in exchange for the short story.

What are you usually found doing when you're not writing?
Reading, watching TV, walking my dog in the beautiful Utah mountains, attending music festivals, and eating yummy food.

What does your writing space look like?
My apartment kitchen! And often my cell phone. But I do want to get back into writing by hand. And, someday, in my own house create a separate library and office space to dedicate to reading and writing.

If you wrote your autobiography, what would you name it?
Chaos in Color

How long did it take to write your novel, and what was your process?
It usually takes me about a month to write a novel from start to finish. I list out some tropes I want to hit, get a cover made or dig in my stash, put 1-3 sentences per chapter, and just start writing. I'm on the panster end of the planner-planster-panster spectrum.

ZEPHRY'S CURSE CONT'D

Favorite reads?
Too many to count, but you can 9/10 find me with an indie romance in my hands.

Do you have any book recommendations?
I would say Delicious Monsters by Liselle Sambury. Has just about everything, addictive style, and finished 500 pages in about three days! Plus, it's YA so while it touches on some very heavy themes, it doesn't go into great enough detail to scar.

What's your next big project?
A lot actually. Join my guild to learn more about all my projects, as well as support me in publishing more diverse romances: https://authorzknight.com/guild

Do you have any advice for aspiring authors?
Just get some words on the page!

HEY JUDE

Kathleen has been a freelance writer since 1999 and now writes full-time.

Her work has appeared in Doll World Magazine, Apolloslyre.com, The Lake County Journals, Trails.com; USA Today (travel), Livestrong.com (lifestyle), Essortment, eHow, Answerbag, Examiner.com, Suite101, and YahooVoices.

She is the author of Heatherstone, the award-winning novels Hey Jude, Tell Me You Love Me, Whispers On A String, and the Head Case Rock Novel Series (Head Case, Whiplash, and Haven).

She also has short stories published in the Secrets: Fact or Fiction I & II anthologies.

Keep in touch

https://m.facebook.com/kathleenstonewriter
https://twitter.com/kstonewriter
https://www.instagram.com/kstonewriter

HEY JUDE CONT'D

When did you start writing?
I started writing as a small child, creating picture books with my own terrible drawings, LOL.

What was it like growing up?
I had a wonderful childhood growing up in the 60s and 70s with my parents and younger sister.

How was your early life?
My dad worked three jobs to put a roof over our head and food on the table, and my mom waitressed two nights a week. Having a stay-at-home mom was the norm in the 60s and 70s, so I spent my early life playing with my cousins and younger sister, and I didn't have a care in the world. My childhood memories are the best.

What has been the biggest influence in your career?
I'd have to say the biggest influence in my career is music. I listen to it pretty much all the time, whether writing or in the car, or cooking dinner, and not only is it inspirational but therapeutic as well. Music is the balm that heals my troubled mind and makes me want to sing at the top of my lungs. So if I'm not listening to music, I'm writing about it somehow.

Tell us about your newest release.
My newest release is Heatherstone, which is my first romantic fantasy novel. It follows the lead character Shelby, as she tries to figure out why she has no memory of her past while evil Master Richard of Heatherstone Castle is quietly pulling the strings to make her his wife.

Which book of yours would you call your favorite child?
That's a tough one, but at the moment, I would have to say, Hey Jude, about a four-year-old deaf boy named Shea and the relationship he develops with his live-in nanny, Jude.

What inspired you to write this book?
I have had the character of Shea in my head for many years, and it was finally the right time for his story to be told.

What are you usually found doing when you're not writing?
When I'm not writing, you can find me reading, dog sitting, and when time and finances allow, I love to travel.

What does your writing space look like?
I sit in a wide leather chair surrounded by books, notebooks, pens, plants, and windows that look out onto our one-acre property.

If you wrote your autobiography, what would you name it?
Dosee Dotes (after a song my mom used to sing to me and my misinterpretation of the lyrics - LOL)

How long did it take to write your novel, and what was your process?
I think it took me about a year to write, proofread, edit, and publish Hey Jude. I am fortunate to be able to write full-time, so I write all day and usually stop around five o'clock or so. With Hey Jude, there was a fire I couldn't extinguish however, so I would write all day, and then after dinner, I would continue until I went to bed.

HEY JUDE CONT'D

Favorite reads?
I'll read anything, but my favorites are classics like Jane Eyre or To Kill a Mockingbird, and I'll devour anything that has a music theme. I love books based on rock bands.

Do you have any book recommendations?
I could go on forever when it comes to recommending books, but right now I'd give a shout out to author Barbara Avon, a multi-genre author who writes romance, horror, psychological horror and time travel. I absolutely love getting lost in one of her books, and she has a lot to choose from.

What's your next big project?
I am currently writing a YA novel about an overweight teenage girl whose family owns the local bakery, and her friendship with the new boy next door, who has synesthesia.

Do you have any advice for aspiring authors?
The best advice I can give is to never, ever give up. There are so many times I thought I wasn't cut out for the writing life, but because I persevered through the rough patches, I have turned my passion--my reason for breathing--into award-winning novels that I am extremely proud of. If I had given up, they would not exist today.

TAKE ME TO CHURCH SERIES BY L.M. ARCHER

L.M. Archer was first drawn to writing as a way to express her feelings when oftentimes, she found that she couldn't say them out loud. That's why her writing is more on the dark side of the romance spectrum. She tends to write in a way that showcases real scenarios and events. Her books tackle mental health, moral values, religion, and other raw and real topics. She is not afraid to make her readers look at the darker side of humanity and question the very foundation of life and existence. The topics in her books can be triggering, but she firmly believes that you need to shed light on certain situations. Keeping them in the dark only hurts more.

Keep In Touch

lmarcheroffical.com
instagram.com/lmarcherbooks
facebook.com/lmarcherbooks

T A K E   M E   T O   C H U R C H   C O N T ' D

When did you start writing?
All of my life really.

What was it like growing up?
I grew up on a holler deep into Appalachia. My family was very poor, oftentimes skipping meals to get by. I was raised in a strict Christian household with deep roots in southern traditions.

How was your early life?
I didn't realize how difficult it was until I grew up and could look back on it differently. Not having indoor plumbing wasn't normal, but I assumed it was at the time. There are a lot of examples like that. I was loved by both of my parents. My dad was an incredibly hard worker, and my mom loved us in the ways she knew how. I had two older sisters. We didn't always get along, and I am very different from them, but we loved each other either way.

What has been the biggest influence in your career?
Growing up in a conservative Christian family with strict beliefs, then going to college to study religion from the lense of an academic. It really flipped my worldview, and I use that in my writing.

Tell us about your newest release.
My most recent release was Gentleness in Sin: Book 4 of the Take me to Church series.

Which book of yours would you call your favorite child?
Paradise in Death: Book 3 of the Take me to Church series

What inspired you to write this book?
The inspiration for the whole series came from my personal experience growing up in a small conservative town with strict Christian parents while trying to navigate my own sexuality through all of that. Many people share this experience with me, and I wrote the series to show them that they aren't alone and that nothing is wrong with them. Religious Trauma is a very real thing that people suffer from, so I was hoping to help heal some of that trauma for them through my own writing. In the series, there are a lot of discussions regarding the Bible, faith, God, and sexuality. I wanted to use my educational background as a tool to guide these discussions so my readers would have a better understanding of something they were taught to believe without question.

What are you usually found doing when you're not writing?
Hanging out with my husband and our two cats. Animal Crossings has become a new obsession for me, then of course, reading.

What does your writing space look like?
I write everywhere I can. Usually, at home, on the couch, with the TV on as background noise.

If you wrote your autobiography, what would you name it?
From Moonshine to Wine: The Story of an Appalachian Girl

How long did it take to write your novel, and what was your process?
It took me 9 months to write the entirety of the Take me to Church series. Some novels take longer, while others don't. My writing process is always the same. I start with a concept. Then I write down themes that will go throughout the book as well as character profiles. Then I start outlining chapters which include a small paragraph about what will happen in the chapters and whose point of view it's from. I write chronologically, so I do not skip around depending on what scene is speaking to me. If I have an idea for a scene that pops into my head, I will write it down and rework the chapters.

TAKE ME TO CHURCH CONT'D

Favorite reads?

Immortals After Dark Series by Kresley Cole helped me fall in love with romance. Necessary Evils Series by Onley James has been a recent favorite of mine.

Do you have any book recommendations?

I loved Neon Gods by Katee Roberts. I haven't finished the entire series yet, but I plan to. I also really enjoyed Delilah Green Doesn't Care by Ashley Herring Blake. If you like Dark Romance, I enjoyed Maahes by Emma Jaye.

What's your next big project?

Currently editing a m/m mafia trilogy. I don't know when the first book will be out yet. It's a dark, spicy romance with lots of twists, turns, and violence. I am also writing an m/m rockstar romance trilogy.

Do you have any advice for aspiring authors?

Write what you want to read, and don't be afraid to explore the unknown. Go places other authors haven't gone.

CUPBOARD BOY

I'm a sixty-year-old ex-serviceman who suffers from PTSD as a result of my abusive childhood and my military service with the Parachute Regiment and other Special Forces units.

I served in Northern Ireland and was also involved in the Battle for Mount Longdon in the Falklands War 1982, where I witnessed, and experienced some very dark moments.

In September of 2011 My PTSD made my life unbearable to the point that I attempted to take my own life. Luckily though for me I had a great GP who immediately arranged for me to spend a couple nights in my local psychiatric unit.

However, it was eight weeks before I was discharged. In 2014 my psychiatrist suggested that if I were to write about my life experience's it may help me with the healing process.

Here is my first book which chronicles my early childhood years.

Keep in touch

www.ptsaunders.co.uk

CUPBOARD BOY CONT'D

When did you start writing?
2015

What was it like growing up?
Terrible

How was your early life?
Full of child abuse and racism

What has been the biggest influence in your career?
My own battle with PTSD

Tell us about your newest release.
Just when you thought a story couldn't get any madder, and it's safe to go back into the library, P T Saunders comes up with a second book in the series. Basic Training II Grounded picks up where the first book Basic Training Flying by The Seat of His Pants, ended. Having attempted to prove that A young Scallywag, Ben Baxter, didn't have it in him to get into the Paras,' Our fly decided to follow Ben throughout the grueling twenty-two-week training course. All was going well until some general swotted our fly just before the pass-off parade. In this book, our fly has been reincarnated into Sgt Maj Brynn Williams and the Sgt Major into a fly somewhat temporarily. Unable to come to terms with his reincarnation, our fly is sectioned under the mental health act. Where he meets a few, let's say interesting Characters, such as Cowboy Dave, Sue, the boxer-short thief, and Spanish, a typically gobby scouser. Upon his release from the hospital, he completes his mission of proving that Ben doesn't have what it takes to be a Para. During that mission, he meets the Bus-Hag, Charlotte, the woman with more with a little extra anatomy, and a couple of drunks he nick-names Bill and Ben, the pissed-up men. Will he succeed in his mission? You'll have to buy the book to find out.

Which book of yours would you call your favorite child?
Me and my Black Dog

What inspired you to write this book?
My Psychiatrist

What are you usually found doing when you're not writing?
I love to walk along the North East coast

What does your writing space look like?
I have converted a small bedroom into my office. However, this year I am going to be building a garden office.

If you wrote your autobiography, what would you name it?
From Fighter to Writer

C U P B O A R D   B O Y   C O N T ' D

How long did it take to write your novel, and what was your process?
It took me about ten months to write. I first wrote notes on my childhood memories and then ran them past my siblings for accuracy. Then I just dived right in there and wrote and re-wrote non-stop. My psychiatrist suggested that when I completed my story, I should symbolically tear it up to rid my memory of the sight and sounds of horrific child abuse. However, as I wrote the book, I realized that people needed to be aware of child abuse and how parents are very clever at covering abuse up.

Favorite reads?
Of Mice and Men, An Inspector Calls The Red and Green Life Machine

Do you have any book recommendations?
I Have a Black Dog by

What's your next big project?
I am currently writing a new revenge thriller, "Re-Set"

Do you have any advice for aspiring authors?
Write, read, and re-write

GAIN LIFE GUIDANCE

Sent to your email for .99

Grow daily insight on what's going on with your personal astrology and numerology, clear chakras and learn how an affirmation adds to your story.

www.wholisticfitnessny.com
healingwithin76@gmail.com

AUTHOR FEATURE

DELPHINE MCCLELLAND

Delphine McClelland was born in Statesville, North Carolina, and graduated from Statesville Senior High School. After graduating from high school, she took her dreams and passions to Knoxville, Tennessee, where she attended and graduated from The University of Tennessee with a degree in Anthropology.

Her career path was set until life happened, and her plans to go to grad school got derailed. After finding a job, her co-worker John Voldstad planted the seed for her to turn her passion for reading into a new passion for writing.

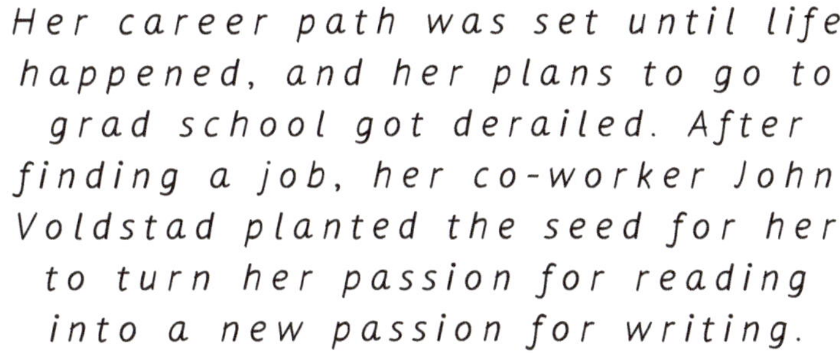

With that new passion, Delphine wrote her first Adult Paranormal Romance Novel, Dark Obsessions, now a two-time Award Winning Book.

Dark Obsessions has won the American Fiction Award as well as winning two Third Place Awards in the BookFest Awards

DELPHINE CONT'D

Delphine is your all-around fun-loving person.

Her family and friends mean the world to her, and their encouragement and push help to make Dark Obsessions a reality

She attends Throne of Grace Church and is a huge Dallas Cowboys and Tennessee Volunteer fan.

She loves all things Stitch and Game of Thrones.

Follow Delphine:

www.delphinemcclelland.com
Facebook
https://www.facebook.com/DLMObsessions IG-delphinemcclelland

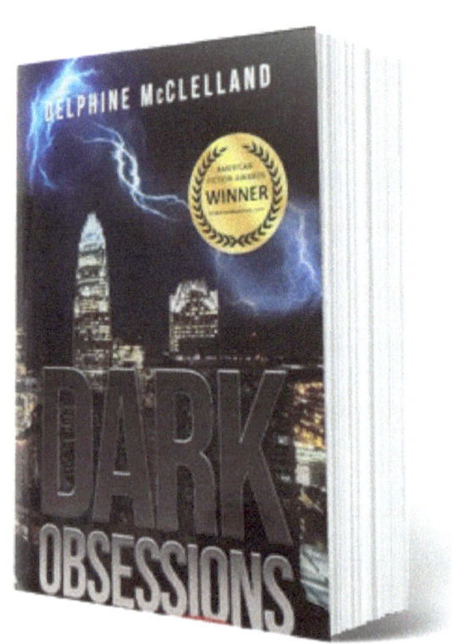

AUTHOR FEATURE

DYLAN BRENNAN

Dylan Brennan is a 16-year-old writing prodigy living in London.

An avid reader, student and musician, Dylan has recently proven his academic excellence with his outstanding GCSE grades, obtaining a phenomenal eleven grade 9s.

An aspiring author, 'Noble: Betrayed' is Dylan's first work and will hopefully launch a promising writing career experimenting with and forming innovations in a wide variety of literary genres.

AUTHOR FEATURE

DYLAN BRENNAN CONT'D

'Noble: Betrayed' is a thought-provoking fusion of the sword-swinging, army-inspiring medieval tales of political intrigue and love and death and honour, and the grounded realism of familial love and the grave consequences that the harrowing history of two can have on society as a whole.

This book may be fantasy, but it's also very real.

At the heart of Brennan's debut novel, and what receives universal praise, is the writing style.

'Noble: Betrayed' revolves around the first-person inner ramblings of a wide array of potentially-unreliable narrators, allowing the reader to piece the story together as they wish and formulate their own interpretations of the societal descent of The Great Kingdom. It is an exceptionally rare style in the epic fantasy genre. It allows for a reading experience like no other as you become engrossed in the sword-swinging, oath-breaking treachery that swarms the sizeable ensemble.

Non-fantasy lovers should find something that interests them too - the novel tackles domestic abuse, familial disharmony, and disability in its Medieval England-esque setting.

Mystery lovers should also have fun picking apart the story of Dayron Pargion, who uncovers an Earth-turning mystery about the true nature of the Kingdom that can spawn mountains of theories.

Brennan is an exciting young writer with a promising future, and all fantasy lovers should give the novel a try.

FOLLOW BRENNAN

INSTAGRAM: @ELBRENNAN51
TIKTOK: @ELBRENNAN51
TWITTER: @ELBRENNAN51

AUTHOR FEATURE

Misty Rogers

Misty has kept a journal since the age of seven, always enamored with the act of documenting life with words on paper.

She dreamed of compiling her journal entries into a biography-style book, later realizing that her life probably wasn't book-worthy.

Throughout the years, Misty has ventured into blogging, running a fun site and YouTube channel during her college years.

Professionally, Misty works in Marketing and has been copywriting for several years.

Misty fell in love with reading at a very young age, devouring novels of all subjects and sizes since she was in elementary school.

Misty's passion for romance developed with Nora Roberts' endless span of novels. She fell hard for forbidden love tropes, like the ones within the Twilight Saga (hey, they were popular when she was in Middle School!).

Misty also appreciates classic literature, especially the works of Edgar Allen Poe.

Misty now loves to find time in her evenings to binge-read romance novels that she finds on the Kindle App or from one of the many physical books she has on the shelves in her home.

Misty Rogers Cont'd

Misty Rogers is an indie author who stumbled onto the scene in 2021 after writing her debut romance novel, Boss Off Limits.

Misty had always enjoyed writing in the form of nonfiction research articles and informational essays and only ventured into creative writing when she was met with a major reading slump.

In early 2021 she was on a mission to find the perfect romance novel, one with all the feels and just the right amount of spice, but she couldn't find one that checked all her boxes – so she wrote one.

In just three months, Misty had a manuscript that represented everything she loved about the romance genre, mixed with a heavy dose of her own life experiences.

The only thing left to do was to figure out how to get it into the hands of readers.

Querying seemed intimidating, so Misty decided to go the self-publishing route. Her design background helped smooth the process, and by December 31st, she had published her first book.

Follow Misty

@mistyrogers_author on Instagram Misty Rogers on Goodreads

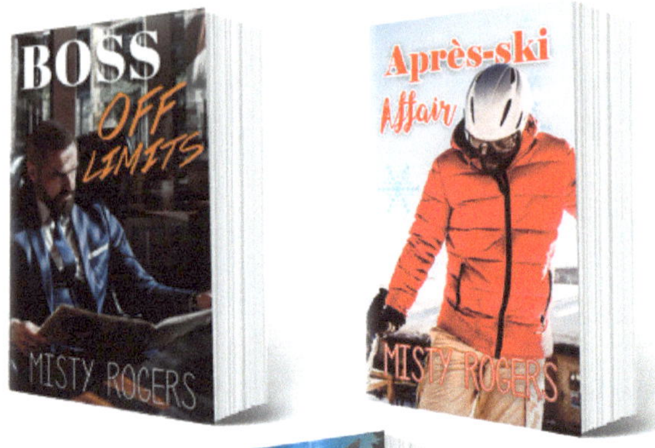

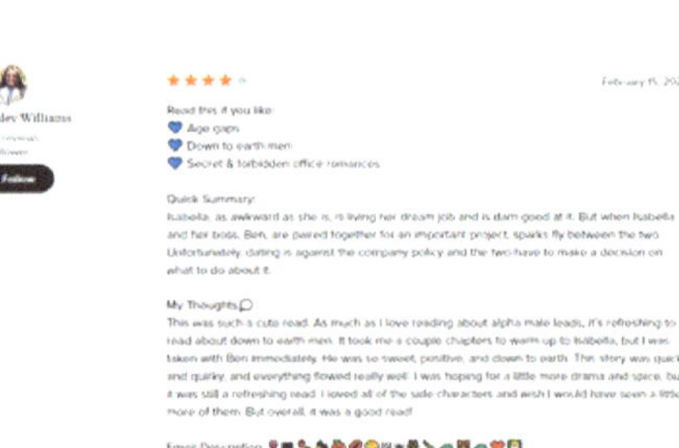

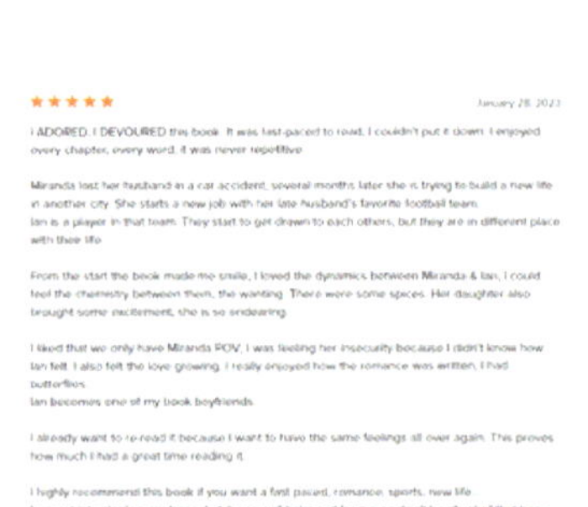

https://mistyrogersauthor.wordpress.com/

AUTHOR FEATURE

ELISE BROOKE

My name is Elise Brooke, and I grew up in Hawkes Bay, NZ. My parents moved to NZ from England and South Africa to create their New Zealand Dream, quickly becoming my New Zealand nightmare.

I have written and published two autobiographies in my book trilogy "The New Zealand Dream," by Sheila, my pen name, here I share about this nightmare,

I wrote these books to inspire and give hope to others. The third and last book in this trilogy is due in April 2023. In 2020 I co-authored a memoir called "Johnathan" by Elise Brooke and Richard Brooke. This is available on Amazon.

My passion is creative writing; I am a certified creative writer and writing coach. I've written for 25 years in fiction, non-fiction, poetry, and content. I have published many articles and guest posted on various sites. I have been featured three times in "The Gisborne Herald" newspaper. The short story "Stargazing," which I won a local award with "Writing Sparks," is loosely based on how I met my husband and moved to Gisborne in 2019.

ELISE BROOKE CONT'D

In 2022 I was featured in the Gisborne writers group anthology called "Katuhi Rawhiti," held in the Gisborne museum and available from Paper Plus and Book depository. Writing is a very powerful healing tool. Sharing your story can help others and help you on your healing journey.

 I am a writing coach who can help people write their own stories or with any writing project they are creating and book marketing. I write on "medium" www.medium.com and "Leveraged writers" www.leveragedwriters.com and Lillian Brummett's "Conscious blog," once a month www.lilliansconsciousblog.com

Follow Elise

https://www.facebook.com/mynewzealanddream

INTERVIEW WITH JAMES IRVING
by Cj Ives Lopez

I had the pleasure of interviewing James twice for The Authors Porch Podcast.

In the first interview, we got to know each other and James' books, and when his publicist came back when his fourth book was releasing, I instantly said yes. The difference this time was that I needed to read more after becoming intrigued by how vividly James painted the picture of his life, career, and imagination.

As he puts it, James's main character Joth Proctor is a culmination of James's career, those he has come in contact with, and an imagination that has no bounds.

A Private detective, a lawyer, and a wonderful mind is the only way this book could be created.

One would think that being a private detective, then a lawyer, and lastly an author is a fictional tale brought to life from someone's mind, but James's fantastical life makes him uniquely qualified to write this series.

I had to ask, and I know you're thinking too, which of his private detective or criminal lawyer stories made it into the book? James's only answer was, "Parts of them, but nothing like the real-life ones, only inspirations from what happens in life."

JAMES V. IRVING
AUTHOR - FRIEND OF THE DEVIL

You may say bummer, but it's even more interesting because the stories are new and exciting, not something already played out inside a courtroom.

Upon reading Friend of The Devil, I realized that the dynamic characters James put together could only live within this series and that I needed to read all of them.

I hope you will find them as intriguing and full of life as I did and read the series. You can find my full review later in the magazine and James typing away as he's almost completed book five.

https://www.jamesvirving.com/

Three Ravens Publishing

Are you looking for fun, new fiction?

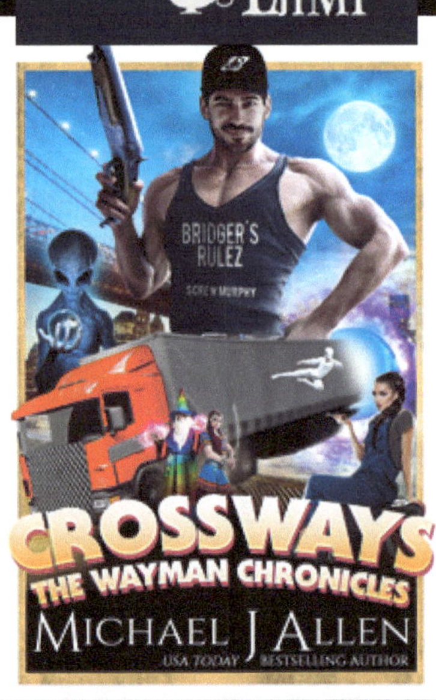

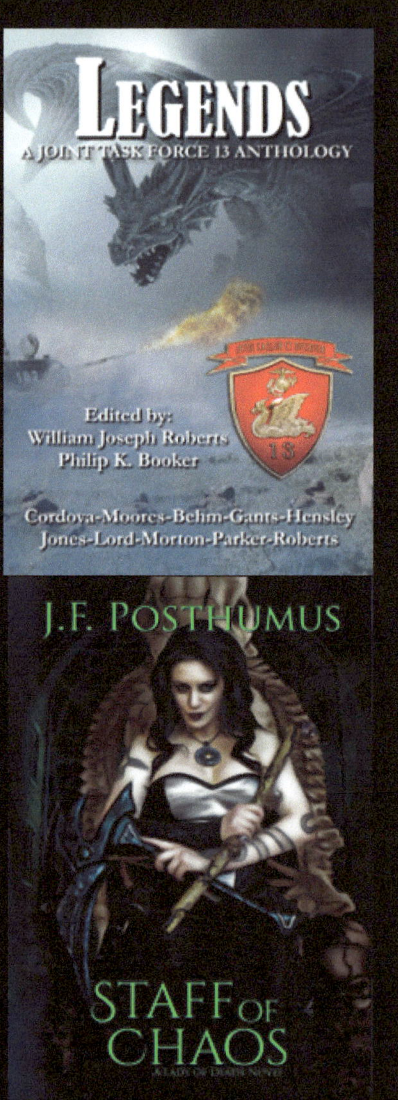

The Written Word Will Never Be The Same…

https://www.threeravenspublishing.com

Veteran Owned and Operated

Joanne's
COSMIC CORNER

Jupiter Enters Taurus: Life Fills with Joy

It's been four months that the planets have been in a Retrograde Free Cycle, but that is about to change.

The Planets Retrograde Cycle begins on April 21, 2023. Starting with Mercury, the planet associated with communication, schedules, transportation, technology, learning, listening, teaching, and contracts, Mercury will retrograde in Taurus from April 21 through May 14. The shadow period begins on April 7th through May 31st

Taurus is associated with physical and material possessions, relationships, and money.

If you have the Sun, Ascending (Rising), Moon, Mercury, or any other planets or the Second House in Taurus this Retrograde may bring up conversations around money and real estate. You may also be reviewing your income.

Venus goes Retrograde in Leo from July 22 through September 3, Venus is the planet of love, sex, beauty, and money. Because Venus deals with both love and money, you can expect unpredictability to come up in both areas of your life

If you have any planets in Leo, the Fifth House, and whatever sign Venus is in on your personal chart during this Retrograde, you may experience anxious energy in your body, which may cause you not to be able to follow up on projects. You may also doubt your relationships and business partnerships. Money will improve.

COSMIC CORNER CONT'D

It is not a good time during Venus Retrograde for any signs to get a makeover, change hair color, get facials, or have surgery.

Jupiter enters Taurus on May 16, 2023, through May 25, 2024.

Jupiter is the planet of expansion and gifts. During this period it is very important for anyone that has Taurus in Sun, Ascending (Rising), Moon signs, 1st, 5th, 6th, or 9th House to schedule daily strength training. Focus on fueling and feeding your body to avoid putting on extra weight.

Uranus will also be in Taurus during this period, which is a rare money cycle. You will be given many new opportunities that will benefit you. This will bring many new changes around you.

Below is the Forecast for all 12 zodiac signs. To benefit from this forecast, I suggest reading the insight for your Sun, Moon and Rising Signs and all other planets associated with each sign on your personal natal chart.

Aries: What a great birthday gift having Jupiter and Uranus sharing energy. Your relationships with money change, and this helps you experience financial freedom. Root, Red, 14 (5) Reverse

Taurus: This month you clean up your financial issues and this will give you a fresh start with money. With Jupiter in Taurus, you may find that you're putting on extra weight, add an extra strength training day to your regimen, or start strength training. Third Eye, Indigo, 17 (8)

Gemini: You will find that your community and relationships are changing, this is helping to match your higher purpose visions. Crown, Purple, 11 (Master Number)

Cancer: You are inspired to socialize more and make new friendships and partnerships. You will also notice that you are more confident; that is Jupiter helping you. Sacral, Orange, 78 (6)

Leo: Venus and Leo's energy do not mix well. You may feel overwhelmed and anxious. This season may be a good time to schedule Reiki or Acupuncture. Know that everything will work out. Sacral, Orange, 9

Virgo: You are inspired to learn something new personally or professionally. This may include travel. You are also making many changes in your life, possibly a new home, job, or community. Heart, Pink, 36 (9)

Libra: You are cleaning house this season. It's important to bring harmony and balance back to your home and body, or else a health issue may come up. Throat, Turquoise, 22 (Master Builder)

Scorpio: This season enhances your spiritual journey with Jupiter and Uranus sharing energy. You start receiving many gifts that may help in discovering who you are on a deeper level. Crown, Purple, 10 (Reverse)

Sagittarius: During Venus Retrograde you are inspired to heal the relationship with your body. This is a perfect time to start strength training, meditation, or take it to the next level. Heart, Green, 34 (7)

COSMIC CORNER CONT'D

Capricorn: As Jupiter enters Taurus you may experience changes in your finances, this helps your business expand or you may even start a business. You may even decide to invest in something. Heart, Green, (00) Reverse

Aquarius: 2023, The Age of Aquarius. This is a great time to build a new foundation. It may look like a new home, business, or a mind, body, and spiritual practice. Sacral, Orange, 96 (6), Reverse

Pisces: This season may give you a chance to expand your career, you have the "How to manual" in your hands. It's important to take care of your feet, ankles, and legs; therefore Reiki or Acupuncture is helpful. Root, Red, 1 (Reverse)
For those of you who have Capricorn, Sun, Moon, Rising, Jupiter, Uranus, Venus or the 10th House on your personal natal chart please redeem your 15 min Complimentary Reiki Treatment on or before May 30, 2023.

In this month's 12-card spread, there were many cards in reverse. There are two reasons why cards are in reverse. The first reason is that guidance is important for you to hear. Also, you may have resistance to the insight, or the chakra may be stuck or blocked.

For questions, comments, or readings, email me at healingwithin76@gmail.com For additional services, go to www.wholisticfitnessny.com

ONCE UPON A BOOK FAIR
JUNE 3RD
10 am to 4 pm
Escondido Center for the Arts
https://jolietunnell.com/once-upon-a-book-fair-2023

Watch the latest episode of The Authors Porch podcast on YouTube or listen on any major podcast platform.

HTTPS://www.youtube.com/@theauthorsporch

CUSTOM BOOK COVER DESIGN BY MIBLART

- Unlimited revisions
- 5 days turnaround
- Pay when you love the result

Poetry Corner

By: Sue Menchell

Fling (Lyrics to a country tune)

I want some quick satisfaction
Not a very long-term thing
Just some kissin' and huggin'
One of those old fashioned flings

Some people say you're too old
Some people say it's no good
All I know is when you hold me
It feels just like it should

I say come on over
You say you can't wait
We don't bother with formalities
We never needed to have a date

I'm just fine with a lover
We don't know if it'll last
Every time we get together
We always have a blast

So, Baby come on over
You don't have to wait
Dress any way you want to
Don't let it get too late

I want some quick satisfaction
Not a very long-term thing
Just some kissin' and huggin'
One of those old fashioned flings

facebook.com/susanjoymenchell; instagram.com/susanjoymenchell

Poetry Corner

By: Sue Menchell

Iron Worker

It's not in the impression left
After the slow hard crawl up in the iron

It's in the mind
Of the man who knows
What all men and women are capable of

It's not in the proof of ability
Or the undeniable repetitions
Of great feats

It's the ability of one's own will
To guide someone
Where they know they're able
And willingly want to go:

This is where the magic is

facebook.com/susanjoymenchell; instagram.com/susanjoymenchell

Poetry Corner

By: Lexi Casidayl

Sleeping Beauty's Castle

A callous has closed over the hole of creativity inside me. There is a deep well of stories which are churning and reaching up through the darkness to make their way out of the cold.

The well where
my stories are trapped lies deep within my heart and are encased by bricks and sandbags, brambles, and brush.

For darkness always leaves behind seeds, and the weeds that grow there are harder to forage through than the spell surrounding Sleeping Beauty's castle.

This churning, this needing to break into my scarred fortress, to let in air, light, and hope; this is the source of all my anxiety.

I want to be seen, but I am scared to see myself, the self that went to sleep to hide from the endless years of beatings, angry words, and flying fists that penetrated deep but not deep enough to
wake the princess at the bottom of the well.

I let her slumber and built thicker walls to keep from disturbing her peace. Now I feel she has been awakened now that we are safe. There are no fists, no screams, no breaking glass. It is safe for her to emerge, and I want to tell her our story. But how do I get through the damn forest I grew to protect her?

IG: @harleyqjitsu youtube: www.youtube.com/@harleyqjitsul

Poetry Corner

By: Lexi Casidayl

Sleeping Beauty's Castle Cont'd

It has been said that the pen is mightier than the sword, and I must believe that this is the tool for the job.

I will tell my stories and clear away the brush with each telling. And with the final telling, I will reach her and offer her a crown jeweled with dignity and pearls.

I will apologize for the dents and tarnish along the journey to reach her. The anxiety will cease, and an oak of elaborate strength will grow out of the well. It awakened the princess. In its shade, she will find solace.

From its leaves, she will heal the wounded around her. From its roots, she will find the courage to stay awake and face the future. And she will thank me for protecting her all this time.

She will don the crown and dissipate into a million little pieces, and everywhere she lands, an oak will grow, whose shade will provide peace so other princesses can come out of hiding and reign as queens.

IG: @harleyqjitsu youtube: www.youtube.com/@harleyqjitsu

Poetry Corner

By: A. Ray

30 Years Time

I don't think of you
As often as I used to
But when I do
I imagine we're 30
And we're catching up over coffee
You're telling me
About the grand adventures
And midnight kisses
While I tell you
About the peace I've found
And how I'm getting better now.

I imagine there would be tenderness
As I reach to hold your hands
I imagine your smile
And how it would make me melt
I imagine your laugh
As I describe all these dreams
That I've kept within me
Recounting all the times
I met you, saw you,
Loved you.

I don't think of you
As often as I used to
Except in the melodies
Of our songs,
In the brisk winds of October,
And sunburnt July,
Tenderly, I think of you,
Most of the time.

And, one day,
Maybe when we're both 30,
And the timing is finally right
My eyes will fall upon yours
The way they did before
And it won't feel like
Starting over
Anymore.

Poetry Corner

By: Elise Smith

Monotonous

*Day in day out I find myself
searching...
Sometimes I know what I am
searching for, other times I have not
a clue on
what to do.
Am I fulfilling my purpose, I was
placed here to fulfill?
Or am I off track once again?
I look for strength, power, comfort,
and a provider.
Most of all I search for answers,
discernment and wisdom are what I
need.
The guidance I long for seems so
hazed.
If I scream would I be heard?
Frustration endures, I am so sick of
being human.
I want to know, but there is little
sign of showing.
Is it today?
Is it tomorrow?
Or another time?
Is this world laughing at me?
It sure seems every time I look to
cross the highway, yet another
vehicle
approaches.
Will I be stuck at this crossroad
forever?*

Ihttps://www.facebook.com/mynewzealanddream

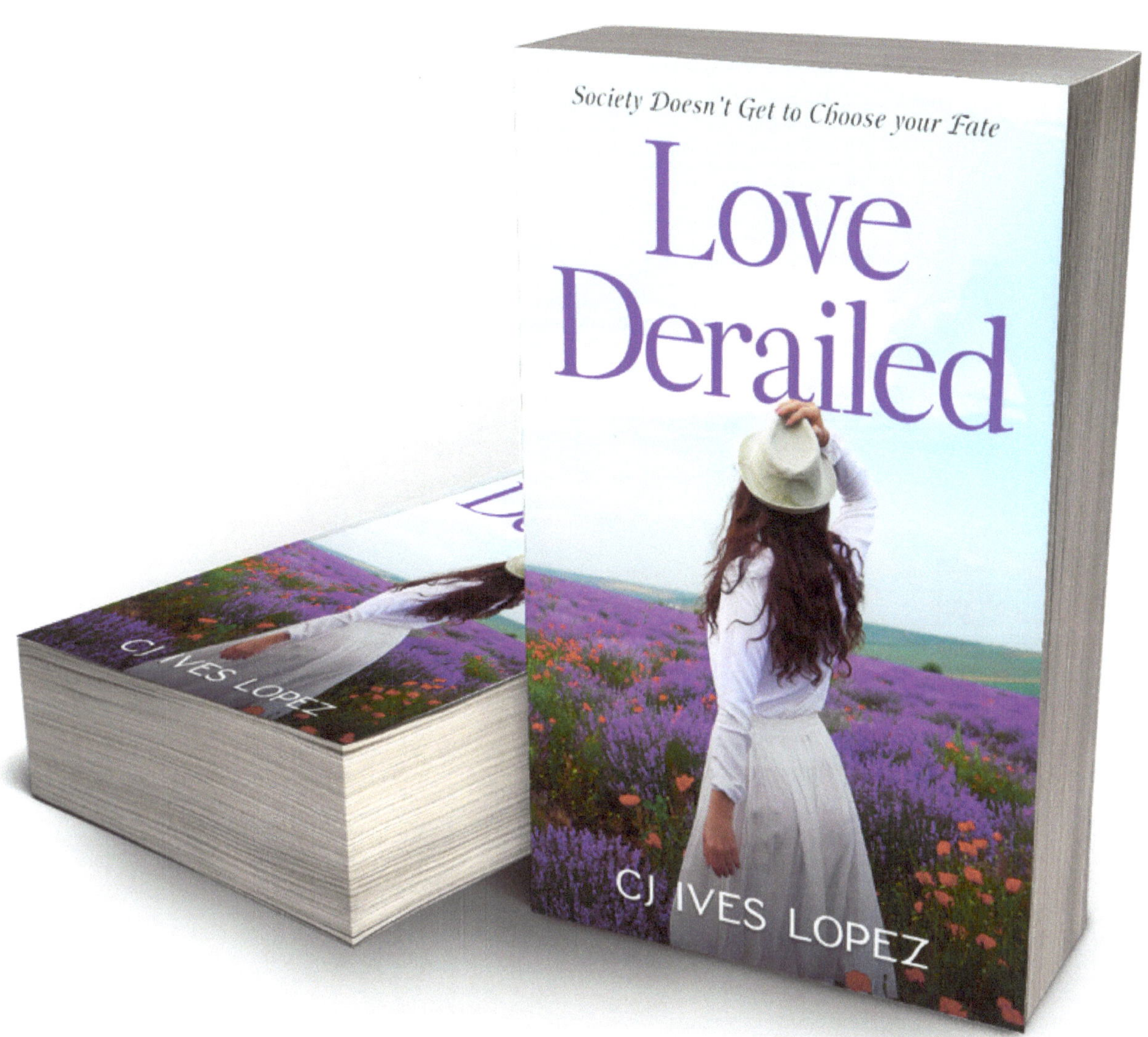

www.cjiveslopez.com

Spring Must Reads

By CJ

There are so many books that it's hard to choose each quarter. I'm glad we have the public to help us with this one.

I went to the public and asked them what we should be reading in the new year, and they did not disappoint.

There are so many different genres out there, and one thing rang true, everyone loves reading, that's for sure.

In the world where digital media is taking over, readers are gonna read.

Here are your New Year's Must Reads, so get to reading, peeps.

CHECKOUT WHATS BLOOMING BEHIND THE PAGES!

Spring Must Reads Cont'd

My First New Year's Must Read is Reckless Beginnings by Tina Hogan Grant.

BOOK ONE OF THE TAMMY MELLOWS TRILOGY

Tammy's had a plan. Move to the U.S. and follow the white picket fence dreams she'd always had. Steven seemed nice, but there were clues she'd missed. He became abusive.
After she had the baby, it got worse.

Steven was addicted to heroin. Thrown into a life of drugs and violence, Tammy lived in fear of what Steven might be capable of and struggled alone to provide for her young son. She longed for any sign of hope. Then he hit her.

You'll be hooked from the beginning because this isn't your typical coming-of-age story, and it's based on true events.

Spring Must Reads Cont'd

Second up,

So I can Grow by Dr. Latarsha Holden is a mini parenting guide that touches on many parenting topics.

Whether you are a new parent, or one who is pulling their hair out, this book will show you that we don't know everything and sometimes we need a helping hand, but it's okay not to know everything.

Spring Must Reads Cont'd

Third up is Sekhet, Book 1 in the Sekhet Saga.

Are you looking for something to make your skin perk up?

Reckoning, Book 2 of the Blackwood Series by J.R. Byers

Molly, unaware of her black powers, summons the red-eyed Hell Demon, Sekhet by accident.

Furious, ready to kill, Sekhet demands Molly make a deal – supply Sekhet with someone to take her place!

Time?

Place?

Sekhet will decide. Molly hides this from her coven and her friends, a fatal mistake. Everyone she loves is now in the Hell Demon's path!

Spring Must Reads Cont'd

Last, but definitely not least is Book one in Tanya Ross's Young Adult Dystopian Tranquility Series.

Sixteen-year-old empath Ember Vinata is devastated by her mother's mysterious death.

But in a disease-free domed metropolis where happiness is electronically monitored and enforced, expressing her grief means exile to The Outside.

The only person who can help her is a smoking-hot government agent.

When strange prophetic dreams compel her to investigate, and she discovers the source of the fatal illness, Ember is stunned to discover the perfect city in which she lives is nothing like it seems. And when her new boyfriend appears to be torn between seeking justice and remaining loyal to his oaths,

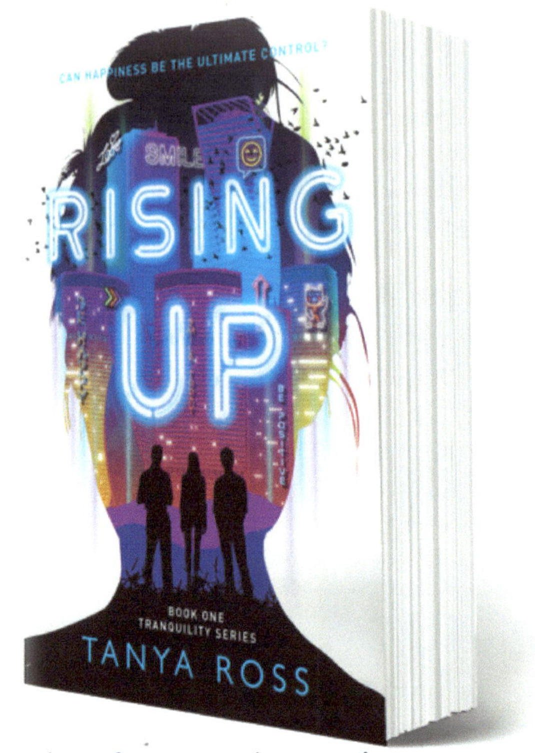

she fears there is no one she can trust...

...Or would her world be rocked by a criminal from The Outside?
Ember's quest for the truth could set her free – or make her a captive pawn. Rising Up is the thrilling first book in The Tranquility YA dystopian sci-fi series. If you like determined heroines, the power of emotions, and fighting injustice, then you'll love Tanya Ross's raw crusade.

Platy
MULTIMEDIA AND PUBLISHING

Promoting literacy one community at a time

Subscribe to our newsletter and we will drop you an email when we go live along with exclusive discounts and new product announcements

34% of Georgia's children are proficient or advanced readers

18% of Brevard County Florida operates at a low level of literacy

70% of New Orleans 2nd graders cannot read at grade level

BENEATH THE SURFACE of the Skin
ALAN LITTLE

Just Like My Dad
By: Elizabeth M. Johnson & Tyrell Plair
ILLUSTRATED BY NICOLAS BADIAA

ELIZABETH JOHNSON AUNTIE MANN
Mamaw Mel's Kitchen

BENEATH THE SURFACE of the Skin
ALAN LITTLE

The Christmas Battle

STOLEN INNOCENCE
TYRELL PLAIR

Igual Que Mi Papá

WWW.PLATYMM.COM

Somebody Like Santa

A Review By: CJ Ives Lopez

Somebody Like Santa by Janet Dailey

My rating: 5 of 5 stars

If you're looking for a perfect Christmas book, this is the one.

Give me a wintery scene in Texas any day, and I'm in. I thoroughly loved this holiday book, and I dug my teeth deep into this beautiful story.

Janet Dailey knows how to keep her readers intrigued throughout the book and to make your heart swoon endlessly. These characters are relatable and fully developed; I wanted them to jump off the pages and become real.

I loved this book and can't wait to see what other stories of Janet's I can sink my teeth into. Grab Somebody Like Santa and hot cocoa, and turn on the Christmas lights. You will have a heartwarming time.

High Achiever

A Review By: CJ Ives Lopez

High Achiever: The Incredible True Story of One Addict's Double Life by Tiffany Jenkins

My rating: 5 of 5 stars

Reading this book, I felt more emotions than I had in a long time. My sister was an addict for over twenty-five years. I never quite understood her journey, but we have talked about it. Reading Tiffany'sbook after following her on social media gives me significant respect for her and the journey to change her life.

My heart broke when she was left to make decisions that no one should ever make. The heartbreak she endured because of addiction and situations no one should go through was gut-wrenching. It's a tragedy when you're in the deepest part of addiction and feel you have no way out.

Many don't realize the grip drugs have on your soul. The rawness of this story is amazingly beautiful. I am so thankful that Tiffany shared so much. There are addicts, family members, and those who have been hurt by an addict that needs to hear this.

The authenticity I felt from this will stay in my heart for years to come, and I would love to listen to a follow-up story of her life now because it is so beautiful.

Friend of The Devil

A Review By: CJ Ives Lopez

"once you have read one, you will want to read them all!"

Friend of The Devil by James Irving

My rating: 5 of 5 stars

I must be upfront that I haven't read the first three books in the series.

Having said that, I am extremely happy to say that the way James has written these books, you can read them stand-alone.

I can also tell you that once you have read one, you will want to read them all.

The characters are fully developed with personalities you can't get enough of. The storylines could be ripped out of the headlines and are full of intrigue and mystery.

I found myself putting down things I needed to get done to find out the next line or paragraph in the book.

While I can't say I've lived in this world, I can see it being played out on a television screen, and I want more.

I had the pleasure of interviewing the author twice, and I'm quite excited for his fifth book to come out.

Josh Proctor may have some scrupulous friends, but their relationships and lives are fascinating.

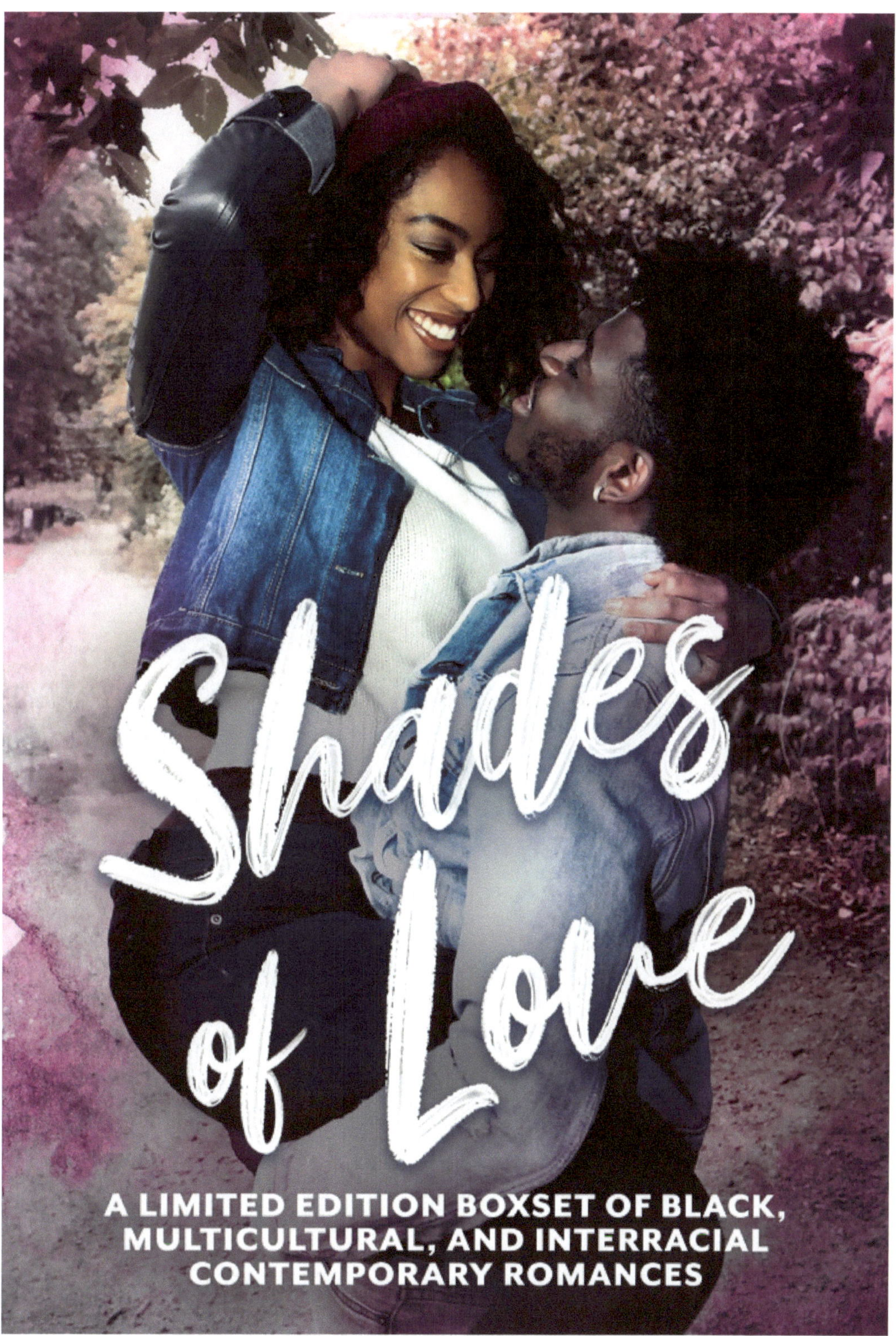
Shades
of Love
A LIMITED EDITION BOXSET OF BLACK,
MULTICULTURAL, AND INTERRACIAL
CONTEMPORARY ROMANCES
www.books2read.com/shadesoflove

About us

Established in 2020 by Retired Air Force Master Sergeant CJ Ives Lopez, and partnered with educator Debbie Covalt Lakin, The Authors Porch is a podcast, Blog, Magazine, and Bookstore to lift literary works and shine the light on authors at every level. They noticed a need to design a space for authors at every height in their careers to join and grow. The Authors' Porch puts authors first and becomes a premier destination for all at every stage in their career. From Live cast to a podcast, blog posts, The Magazine and most recently, The Bookstore situated on the Square in Danville Indiana, The Authors' Porch becomes a beacon of light, drawing you home to a porch where your family is standing by to usher you into your greatness.

1 page = $250

3 graphics
250 words
we will design the ad

1/2 page = $150

2 graphics
100 words
we will design the ad

1/4 page = $75

1 graphic
50 words
we will design the ad

Contact Us

www.theauthorsporch.com
theauthorsporch@gmail.com

www.ingramcontent.com/pod-product-compliance
Lightning Source LLC
Chambersburg PA
CBHW040141240726
48664CB00002B/561